AMICUS ILLUSTRATED • AMICUS INK

DO YOU REALLY WANT TO MEET
AN ORCA?

WRITTEN BY BRIDGET HEOS   ILLUSTRATED BY DANIELE FABBRI

Amicus Illustrated and Amicus Ink
are imprints of Amicus
P.O. Box 1329
Mankato, MN 56002

Library of Congress Cataloging-in-Publication Data
Heos, Bridget, author.
 Do you really want to meet an orca? / by Bridget Heos ; illustrated by Daniele Fabbri.
      pages cm. — (Do you really want to meet... wild animals?)
 Audience: K to grade 3.
 Summary: "A girl goes to the coast of Norway to view killer whales in the ocean and observes their behavior in pods" — Provided by publisher.
 ISBN 978-1-60753-947-6 (library binding) —
ISBN 978-1-68152-118-3 (pbk.) —
ISBN 978-1-68151-065-1 (ebook)
 1. Killer whale—Juvenile literature. 2. Killer whale—Behavior—Juvenile literature. I. Fabbri, Daniele, 1978– illustrator. II. Title.
 QL737.C432H456 2016
 599.53'6—dc23   2015029358

Editor: Rebecca Glaser
Designer : Kathleen Petelinsek

Printed in the United States of America at Corporate Graphics in North Mankato, Minnesota.

HC 10 9 8 7 6 5 4 3 2 1
PB 10 9 8 7 6 5 4 3 2 1

ABOUT THE AUTHOR

Bridget Heos lives in Kansas City with her husband, four children, and an extremely dangerous cat . . . to mice, anyway. She has written more than 80 books for children, including many about animals. Find out more about her at www.authorbridgetheos.com.

ABOUT THE ILLUSTRATOR

Daniele Fabbri was born in Ravenna, Italy, in 1978. He graduated from Istituto Europeo di Design in Milan, Italy, and started his career as a cartoon animator, storyboarder, and background designer for animated series. He has worked as a freelance illustrator since 2003, collaborating with international publishers and advertising agencies.

So you think you'd like to meet an orca. Did you know they are called killer whales because they kill and eat sharks, seals, and even whales much bigger than them?

Orcas hunt as a pack, surrounding animals and
chasing them at speeds of 34 miles (55 km) per hour.
Then orcas sink their giant teeth into their prey.

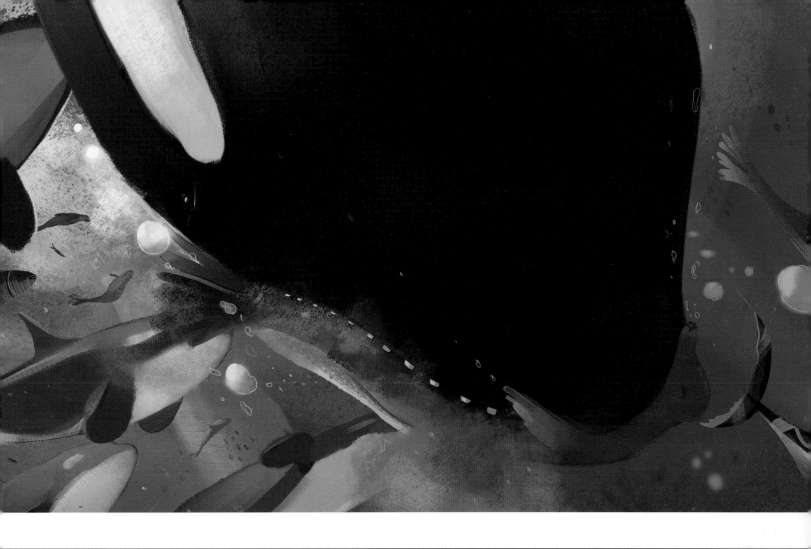

They are not actually whales. Orcas are the largest
type of dolphin—and they are awesome predators.
Do you *really* want to meet one in the wild?

You do? Okay, let's go. Orcas live in all the world's oceans.
But they prefer cold water, like on the coast of Norway.
Bring a pillow. The flight to Norway will take all night.

All aboard! We're going to spend five
days on board a ship—chasing orcas!

Whoa! That orca is huge. Orcas can weigh up to 17,600 pounds (8,000 kg). Since orcas are mammals, they must come up for air. They breathe through their blowholes.

Sometimes lots of orcas come up for air at the same time. This is an orca pod, or family. A pod can have 5 to 50 orcas. There are babies, mothers, older sons and daughters, grandmothers, and more. Orca dads are usually from other pods.

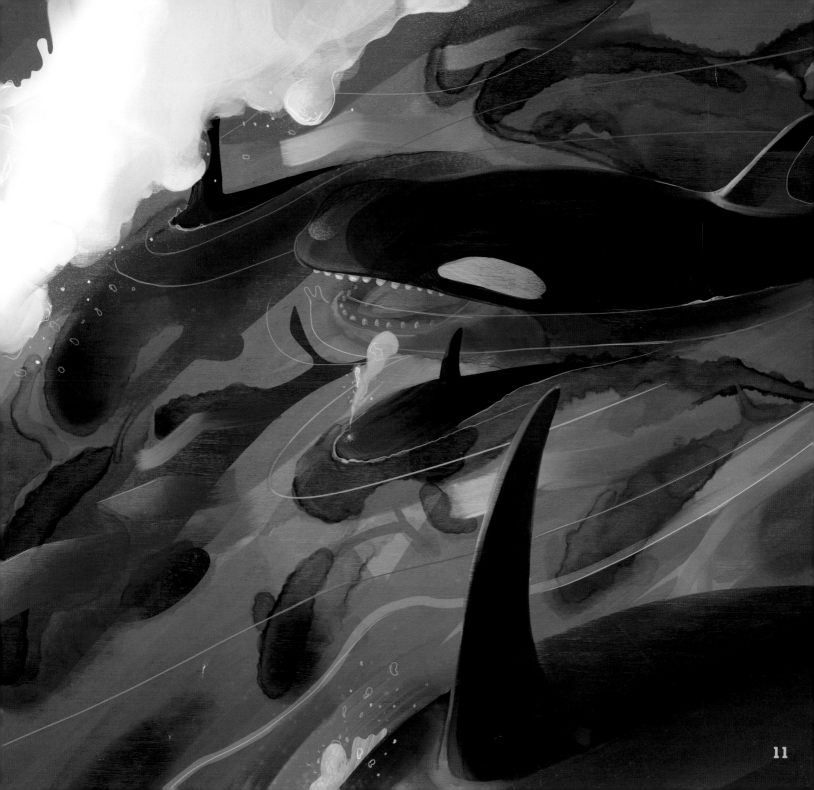

Do you want to meet the family? You've taken
scuba diving lessons, right? Then dive in!

Hey, where did they go? Orcas
can be hard to see underwater.

That's because their black and white skin is camouflage.
From above, the black blends in with the dark ocean.

From below, the white blends in with the sunlight.
This allows the orca to sneak up on its prey.

There's an orca! Wait a second. Why is it opening its mouth? Orcas that hunt mammals might mistake a human for a seal. But orcas don't usually attack humans in the wild. Better watch from a distance, just to be safe!

Don't worry. This orca isn't hunting for mammals at all! Orcas that live in big family groups, like this one, mainly eat fish like herring. Yum!

Look, a little orca! Mothers and other family members care for baby orcas and teach them how to "talk."

Orcas communicate by whistling to each other. I think the orcas are saying hello. Hi, orcas!

MAP KEY

⬤ Orcas

GLOSSARY

blowhole A hole on the top of an orca's or other dolphin or whale's head through which it breathes.

camouflage Coloring on an animal's skin that helps it blend in with its surroundings.

mammal An animal that has fur (if only a tiny bit at birth), is warm-blooded, and drinks its mother's milk.

pack A group of animals that hunts together.

pod A group of orcas or other marine animals.

predator An animal that hunts other animals for food.

prey An animal that is hunted for food.

READ MORE

Allyn, Daisy. *Killer Whales Are Not Whales!* New York: Gareth Stevens Publishing, 2015.

Drumlin, Sam. *Orcas.* New York: PowerKids Press, 2013.

Hodson, Sally. **Granny's Clan: A Tale of Wild Orcas.** Nevada City, Calif.: Dawn Publications, 2012.

Riggs, Kate. *Killer Whales.* Mankato, Minn.: Creative Education, 2012.

WEBSITES

Explore: Oceans: Orcas
http://explore.org/videos/player/orcas
Meet scientists who study orcas and see amazing shots of orcas in the ocean in this short video.

Kids Do Ecology: Marine Mammals: Orca
http://kids.nceas.ucsb.edu/mmp/orca.html
This is a great resource for report writers about the basics of orca life.

National Geographic Kids: Orca
http://kids.nationalgeographic.com/animals/orca/
Fun facts about orcas, from visual size comparisons and scientific classification to videos and photos.

National Wildlife Federation: Kids: Ooh... Orcas!
http://www.nwf.org/Kids/Ranger-Rick/Animals/Mammals/Orcas.aspx
Read more about how orcas behave in the wild and see orca photographs.

Every effort has been made to ensure that these websites are appropriate for children. However, because of the nature of the Internet, it is impossible to guarantee that these sites will remain active indefinitely or that their contents will not be altered.